128 BEATS PER MINUTE

DIPLO

UNIVERSE

First published in the United States of America in 2012
by UNIVERSE PUBLISHING

A Division of

Rizzoli International Publications, Inc.
300 Park Avenue South
New York, New York 10010
www.rizzoliusa.com

Design by Colin Tunstall

Edited by Leah Whisler

Creative Direction by Jamie McPhee and Kevin Kusatsu

2012 2013 2014 2015 2016 / 10 9 8 7 6 5 4 3 2 1

Printed in China

Library of Congress Catalog Control Number: 2011940111

ISBN: 978-0-7893-2428-3

WWW.MADDECENT.COM
WWW.FACEBOOK.COM/DIPLO
WWW.SHANEMcCAULEY.COM
WWW.SHANEMcCAULEY.TUMBLR.COM

Front cover: Ibiza, 2010.
Back cover: Club Blue in Mexico City, 2011.

CONTENTS

<<< **ALL PLAYLISTS CURATED BY DIPLO**

DEDICATION

In 2003 *Fader* magazine asked my friend, the promoter and independent music ambassador Sean Agnew, what was happening in Philadelphia. He mentioned a few indie bands and artists and also said that the magazine should check out Hollertronix, a new underground party that was creating a lot of buzz for its unorthodox style of DJing.

Photographer Shane McCauley was the local hired hand, and he thought it would be the perfect first time to shoot a party. Party photography wasn't that common, and even though Shane mostly shot bands at the time, he was into the idea. He had been to the party a few times and knew he had to take some towels to keep his lens from fogging up.

Five years later, the label Mad Decent had been initiated, and we got a permit from the city of Philadelphia for $10, and eighty signatures to section off two blocks in front of The Mausoleum, my studio on 12th and Spring Garden. The night before, I was reacquainted with Shane, who was in town and available to shoot pictures of our first party.

Seven years, thirty-two countries, sixty thousand photos, and a million miles later, here is what we've been doing. This book is a living document of parts of my life, job, and travels, as seen through Shane's eyes. It is as much his book as it is mine.

—DIPLO

@diplo

ELPHIA

I guess I moved to Philadelphia because I couldn't afford to live in New York or Los Angeles or San Francisco. Those cities are your first choices if you're an artist, right? It's sort of like I threw a dart at a US map and it just landed there— in a town with cheap rent, limited aspirations, and a lot of empty lots. I never thought it would be a blessing to begin a movement there. Philly's a city with no movement, like still water on a damned creek. It's a bootleg New York, with all the grime, glitter, and strife—but there's no glamour and no gold.

My first year there, Allen Iverson rented the Gallery, a mall downtown, for a party during All-Star weekend, which I snuck into by way of the loading dock. Back then, I would jump fences to swim in public pools late at night and go to warehouse parties north of Susquehanna Avenue to do nitrous with hippies or guys recently released from state prison. I wanted to make music, to DJ, to do something, but no one was buying into my vivid dreams. I met DJ Low Budget at the North Star Bar. He already had a foothold in the hip-hop scene, but both of us were into this new sound— Baltimore club, eighties throwbacks, and even something called mash-ups. When I tell the story of Hollertronix now, it's not so exciting to play these sounds, but back in 2004, it felt like a revolutionary attitude.

Previous spread:
The first Mad Decent Block Party, 2008.

Right: DJ Sega is a native Philadelphian DJ and producer. His father, DJ Brother Rob, raised him on classic soul and R & B. By the time Sega was nineteen, he was holding a weekly party, playing Baltimore club at a local roller rink.
@djsega

Above: Hollertronix, 2003. Diplo + his partner DJ Low Budget (aka Mike Maguire) held their original party in the basement of a Ukrainian club in Philadelphia. The Hollertronix party was the first of its kind in the US. It blended elements of every genre of hip-hop with the fledgling indie rock movement, classic eighties, new wave, and more. It defined a new movement within the club environment. *@lowbeezy*

Above: Diplo + DJ Low Budget back in the day (2005).
Below: Diplo + DJ Low Budget now (2011)—the first they'd worked together in over five years.

Above: Maluca + Amanda Blank double-dutch at the Mad Decent Block Party, 2008. Blank is an artist involved in many different aspects of the local Philadelphia scene. She is a member of a performance-art troupe called Sweatheart, has performed at the gallery Space 1026, and has a solo music career (her debut album, *I Love You*, samples a variety of influences, including LL Cool J's "I Need Love" and Romeo Void's "Never Say Never"). Maluca is a Dominican-American performer who became a friend through various party promoters in New York City. One day an e-mail appeared in her in-box with a song that Diplo wanted her to record, and in the summer of 2009, Mad Decent released her first single, "El Tigeraso." *@SpankAndBlank @MALUCAMALA*

Right: The first
Mad Decent Block
Party, 2008.

Above: Mad Decent Block Party, 2008.

PHILADELPHIA
PLAYLIST

1. CAJMERE
"Percolator"

2. MENAGE A TROIS
"Funky 69"

3. TYLER THE CREATOR
"Yonkers"

4. K-SPIN
"Fight Em" (remix)

5. TV ON THE RADIO
"Staring at the Sun"

6. BONE CRUSHER
"Never Scared"

7. THE PRODIGY
"Smack My Bitch Up"

8. PETER BJORN AND JOHN
"Young Folks"

9. GREEN VELVET
"Shake and Pop"

10. PEEDI CRAKK
"Fall Back"

Above: Rye Rye at age seventeen, 2008. A performer from Baltimore, Rye Rye was introduced to Diplo by DJ Blaqstarr, who ended up producing "Shake It to the Ground," her first single for Mad Decent, when she was just seventeen. She is currently signed to Interscope and has released various singles through the label. @RyeRye

Right: Down on the ground at the Mad Decent Block Party, 2008.

Above: DJ Sega, 2010.

Opposite, top left: Maluca on the mic. **Top right:** Bosco Delrey + Bunny. **Bottom (from left):** DJ Sega, Leejone Wong, Derek Allen, Jasper Goggins, Mike Woodward, Paul Devro, Kevin Kusatsu, Nick Devey, Bosco Delrey, Bunny, Diplo, and Zeb + Shoaib from POPO. This photo is from the third Mad Decent Block Party, which was held in 2010. This was the first time that everyone involved with the label congregated in Philadelphia for the event. This was also the first year the Block Parties went national and were held in three other North American cities. *@derekallen812 @jaspergoggins @benzona @pauldevro @kevinkusatsu @theV @boscodelrey @diplo @zebsdead*

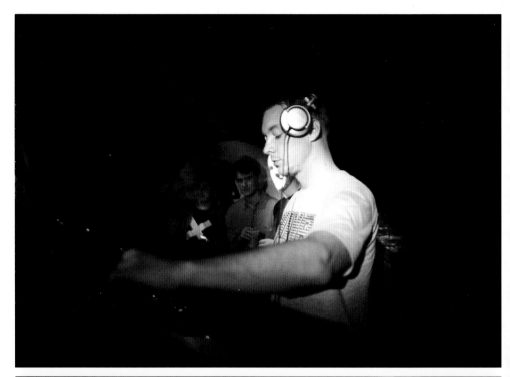

Top: Diplo with Ezra Koenig + Rostam Batmanglij of Vampire Weekend at Voyeur, 2010. *@arzE @matsoR @vampireweekend*

Bottom: Starlight Ballroom, 2010.

Right: Diplo + life-size Diplo at Spring Jam, Drexel University, 2011.

Top left: MC Elixir is a Philadelphia MC that hosted the original Hollertronix parties. These photos are from the summer 2011 Hollertronix reunion party at the Barbary, located in Fishtown in Philadelphia. It was the first time in five years that Low Budget + Diplo played together. *@MCElixir @TheBarbary*

Bottom right: Shortly after this photo was taken, an inebriated attendee ran up from behind the DJ booth and flipped over the table for no apparent reason. It took about three minutes to get everything back up and running again.

EUR

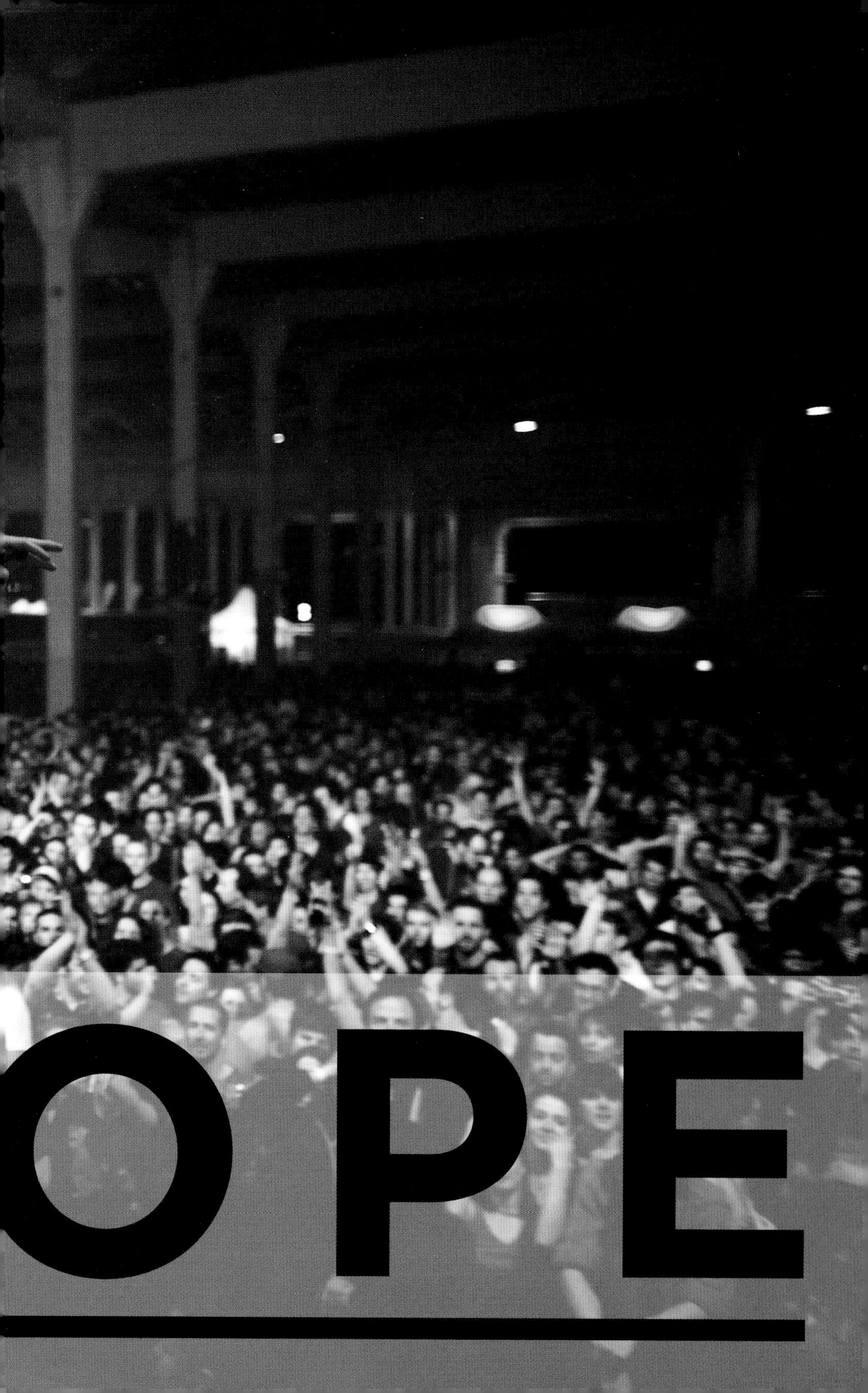
OPE

Europe is the size of America but its cultural variations are one hundred times as vast. One day you're in Paris, then you're in Berlin, then Rome, then Ibiza, and on and on. Every city has its own cultural movement, history, fashion, and art—all of which is constantly evolving into something different. No matter where I go, I feel like the crew of DJs and musicians I'm touring with— a bunch of kids from north London in Paris, a crew from New York in Amsterdam, Swedish kids at a festival in Geneva—are part of a new cultural language. Every time it gets closer to a family reunion or a neighborhood barbecue.

I do a lot of exploring because I'm forced to in some of the places that I end up. I might have only ten hours before a show and the flight to the next place, but my mind is racing. I want to go get lost. One of the clubs I play is five blocks from the Arc de Triomphe in Paris while another, in Ibiza, is located about a five-minute walk from a secret beach. In one of these photos, I'm DJing in Barcelona in an underground car park at a festival called Primavera. The car park is right on the Mediterranean. There were twenty thousand people who came to my set at 4:00 a.m., and I finished as the sun was coming up. Moments like these keep me from feeling so foreign.

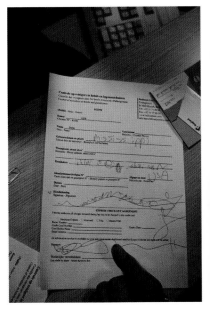

Previous spread: Diplo at Primavera Sound Festival, Barcelona, 2010.

Above: View of Barcelona from the hotel.

Left: Hotel desk in Belgium, 2008. Diplo's signature and an enduring fascination with dinosaurs.

Right: Diplo in Brussels, 2008.

Every city has its own cultural movement, history, fashion, and art. It's constantly developing into something different.

Diplo + Erol Alkan, Pukkelpop, 2008. Most DJ setups at large festivals include two turntables, four CDJs (a CD player built specifically for DJing), and two mixers to transition smoothly between DJs throughout the night. One of the several technologies available to DJs today is shown here—the Serato Control vinyl record in green. Serato, known for trying to bridge the divide between the versatility of digital audio and the tactile control of vinyl turntablism, produces many popular digital DJing tools. The green records pictured here pick up the frequency within software and output in an analog tone where the timing of the music is picked up within the groove of the records.

Above: Erol Alkan.
More about Erol, page 35.

EUROPE
PLAYLIST

1. MARBLE PLAYERS
   "Marble Anthem"

2. TIËSTO vs DIPLO
   "C'mon"

3. JUSTICE
   "Waters of Nazareth"

4. ZOMBIE NATION
   "Kernkraft 400"

5. M.I.A.
   "XR2"

6. STROMAE
   "Alors en Danse"

7. CROOKERS
   "Love to Edit"

8. SONIC C
   "Stickin'"

9. OUI'WACK
   "Jungle Wars"

10. DJ DLG
    "Paramount" (Rogerseventytwo remix)

In the lobby of a Belgian Radisson the day after performing the Pukkelpop festival with A-Trak, 2008. A-Trak is a Montreal-born DJ and producer. At fifteen, he won the DMC DJ World Championship—the world's largest DJ competition. Since then he has toured the world extensively and, at one point, was

recruited by Kanye West to be his touring DJ. He is currently based in New York where he runs Fool's Gold Records, a label that has broken several artists over the past few years, including Kid Cudi, Kid Sister, and Duck Sauce. His older brother Dave is half of the group Chromeo. foolsgoldrecs.com *@atrak*

This spread: Brodinski (left, backstage, and right, onstage, at the Pukkelpop festival, Belgium, 2008) is a French-born DJ + producer (his full name is Louis Roge). He is a resident of the dance club/venue Social Club, which is located in Paris. Social Club is an epicenter for fledgling local dance-music artists. *@Brodinski*

From page 30: Erol Alkan is an English DJ of Turkish-Cypriot descent. He was the founder and host of a weekly party in London called Trash, which ran from 1997 to 2007. Erol was instrumental in propelling new music genres forward within the London club scene. Most of the popular bands of that time played at his club—acts like LCD Soundsystem, Klaxons, Bloc Party, Yeah Yeah Yeahs, and Electric Six. The significance of Trash and how it affected London will remain a legacy within the history of modern music for years to come. Erol also founded the label Phantasy Sound and enjoys success as a music producer of artists in dance, rock, and more. For information about the history of Trash, visit www.trashclub.co.uk. *@erolalkan*

Top: Matt + Kim with Diplo, Amsterdam, 2010. Matt + Kim are a Brooklyn duo who also happen to be married. Matt plays keyboard, Kim plays drums, and they both sing. Kim has a very healthy obsession with hip-hop and R & B. Their show has an incredibly energetic spirit, which is only amplified by the enthusiasm of their fans. It is truly a sight to see. *@mattandkim* **Bottom:** Clubgoers, Bordeaux, 2011.

Right: Skerrit Bwoy, Amsterdam, 2010. Skerrit is an Antiguan national and Major Lazer's MC. When he's not on the road, he can be found in out-of-the-way Caribbean clubs in the Bronx and Brooklyn. *@skerritbwoy*

Above: Joker, Barcelona, 2010. Joker is a grime/dubstep DJ + producer out of Bristol in the UK.
@Joker

Left: Diplo in
the Netherlands
at the Lowlands
festival, 2008.

Top: Colin Stutz, Boy 8-Bit + Diplo outside the Coliseum in Rome, 2009. Stutz was a former tour manager for Diplo. *@colinstutz*

Bottom: Diplo, Rome, 2009. These photos are from a show that was part of a tour with the Italian DJ duo Crookers.

Left: Boy 8-Bit backstage, Rome, 2009. Boy 8-Bit is an English producer + DJ who has released various singles on the Mad Decent label. He's really into heavy metal. *@boy8bit*

Above: Brussels, 2008.

Ibiza, 2010. This is a private, locals-only beach in Ibiza. A local brought everyone touring with Diplo here because of the spot's quiet and remote nature. There are several places to cliff-dive into the Mediterranean.

Above: Maude, Bordeaux, 2011.

Above: Geneva, 2011. **Right:** Dillon Francis, Amsterdam, 2011. Francis is the newest addition to the Mad Decent family. A twenty-three-year-old producer from Los Angeles, he continually sent in music to the Mad Decent general e-mail and SoundCloud page until he was signed a few months later. *@DILLONFRANCIS*

No matter where I go, Barcelona, Liverpool, Berlin, I feel like the crew of DJs and musicians I'm touring with are part of a new cultural language.

Above: Borgore with three computers. Borgore is an Israeli DJ + producer from Tel Aviv. He has served in the military and is also an accomplished saxophone player who studied music composition throughout his schooling. Before carving out a sound in electronic music, he was the drummer in a death metal band called Shabira. *@Borgore*

Left: Borgore + Diplo in the studio, Geneva, 2011.

Above: Diplo ironing before a show, Geneva, 2011. **Right:** David + Stephen DeWaele of Soulwax at Hard L.A., 2010. The duo, who moonlights as 2 Many DJs, is originally from Ghent, Belgium. Soulwax released their first album in 1994 and set the bar for combining progressive rock with electronics and programming. In 2006 they released *Nite Versions*, which has become a somewhat seminal album within the dance/rock hybrid space. 2 Many DJs emerged from the band effort with sets ranging from electro to the classic punk of the Clash. The two are also accomplished app developers, having recently released *This Is Radio Soulwax*. *@soulwax @2manydjs*

This spread: Blaya + Kalaf, Geneva, 2011. Blaya **(above)** + Kalaf **(right)** of Buraka Som Sistema. BSS is a Portuguese group that fuses African Kuduro with electronic music. The group generally performs with a live drummer, two DJs, and Kalaf + Blaya. They had a number one single in Portugal and Spain called "Kalemba (Wegue-Wegue)." *@buraka @kalaf*

Top: Gold fronts, Madrid, 2011. Andrea del Gato, a friend of Zombie Kids.

Bottom: At the Sala, a club in Madrid, 2011.

Right: Brunettes backstage, Madrid, 2011.

Next spread: The Zombie Kids are from Madrid and play very aggressive DJ sets that span hard rock, dubstep, hip-hop, and metal. They're a collective working within the spaces of graphic design, music, and visual art. *@thezombiekids*

ISR

Tel Aviv is not what you might think it is from what you see in the news. It's very secular and wild, with deep historical roots in many different faiths from around the world. Israel is so tiny that you can drive across it in about five hours.

Maybe it's the mandatory military service in the most volatile area of the world, but Israeli kids party like there's no tomorrow. They're absolutely manic. Of all the places I've toured, the cultural complexities of Israel are the most bizarre. One of my first international shows was in Tel Aviv, which is one of the most mysterious cities I know, maybe because of the random soup of reggae, trance, and heavy metal fans. None of the drama you see on Fox News and CNN is visible, but it's a ghostly city that's complex and hard to understand. The most interesting and wild artists I know call it home.

Previous spread:
View of East Jerusalem, 2008.

Right: Diplo in the Old City Jerusalem, 2008.

Above: The Mount of Olives, 2008.

ISRAEL
PLAYLIST

1. WARRIOR QUEEN
   "Check It" (Skream mix)

2. THE CHEMICAL BROTHERS
   "Saturate"

3. COLLIE BUDDZ
   "Come Around"

4. BOOKA SHADE vs M.A.W.
   "Mandarine Girl/Work"

5. BORGORE/DIPLO
   "Sunsets"

6. MAJOR LAZER
   "Cash Flow" (Subskrpt remix)

7. CHASE & STATUS
   "Eastern Jam"

8. UFFIE
   "Pop the Glock"

9. FLUX PAVILION
   "I Can't Stop"

10. MR. VEGAS
    "Lean Wid It"

Top: Friends take Diplo to the Dead Sea, 2008.
Bottom: Diplo midday in 110-degree weather, 2008.
Right: Diplo in Jerusalem, 2008.

Tel Aviv Beach, 2008.

This spread: Before and after mudding in the Dead Sea. Because of its mineral-rich mud, the Dead Sea is thought to have therapeutic and detoxifying effects.

Maybe it's the mandatory military service in the most volatile area of the world, but Israeli kids party like there's no tomorrow...absolutely manic.

This spread: Barzilay Club, Tel Aviv. This club in an outlying area of Tel Aviv is literally underground and has a very racy element to it. There is no mistaking that you're in a dance club, but the feel inside is so secular you wouldn't really know you're in Israel unless you were all talking.

JAM

You know, I started out playing in my neighborhood bar for free dinners and a cut of the bar, sometimes taking home just $20 or $30. I would take any gig that came up once I quit my day job. It wasn't always easy to make ends meet. An offer came in to DJ on a cruise ship for hippies called Jam Cruise, with bands and has-been DJs. The boat went deep into the Caribbean, and I ditched it in Ocho Rios, Jamaica. My friend had come along with me, and we decided that we would not get back on the boat. Instead, we made our way to Kingston because I wanted to record some music there.

This was the advent of the Major Lazer project, a collaboration between me + Switch and various vocalists. It has recently extended beyond its Jamaican influence but is still rooted in the modern dancehall sound. We got a taxi at a gas station to take us over the Blue Mountains for $60. The driver blasted Kenny Rogers and Backstreet Boys live cassettes from his modified trunk subwoofers. We thought he might have done that for us, but it turned out that these were his favorite albums. I knew from this trip on that my perception of Jamaica was going to be shattered.

Major Lazer wasn't a name until two years later, but my journeys through Jamaica have been pretty thorough, from uptown nightclubs to the countryside, from sugarcane fields to high-tech studios to closets with Radio Shack mics and boom boxes. It's hard to experience in pictures what Kingston and the rest of the island is like, but this is pretty close. Jamaica is all music, everywhere, mashed up into one dense curry. Everyone seems to be inspired, the parties are massive, and the innovation is the highest and strangest in the world. In one way or another, every genre I work in now has its roots in this island.

Previous spread: Diplo at Strawberry Hill in Jamaica's Blue Mountains, 2009. Strawberry Hill is a famous hotel owned by Chris Blackwell, the founder of Island Records.

Opposite: Passa Passa street party, Kingston, 2009.

This and following spread: Passa Passa street party, Kingston, 2009. A road in Tivoli Gardens, a small Spanish neighborhood in West Kingston, is home to Passa Passa, one of the world's most famous dancehall parties. Weddy Weddy Wednesday, started on Ash Wednesday in 2003, is a weekly party held at Stone Love Headquarters in Kingston. A precursor to Passa Passa, which you will see

more of on the following pages, Weddy Weddy runs from about 11:00 p.m. to 3:00 a.m. Passa Passa takes over at 4:00 a.m. and goes well into the rest of the morning. It is commonly accepted that this gathering helps to bridge gaps in the community, which was once a war zone, and to keep tempers at peace. It has been imitated from Panama all the way to Japan.

Dancehall fashion at Weddy Weddy.

Above: Major Lazer performs on HYPE! TV, a Caribbean television network, 2009. HYPE! TV is like MTV or BET except that it pretty much only broadcasts music. The show is exactly what you see in this photo: People dance and play records.

Right: Kingston dancehall fashion. The locals drink energy drinks and stay up all night, dancing in the streets to the largest speaker rigs you have ever seen.

Following spread

Top left: Studio One, described as the "Motown of Jamaica," is one of reggae's most legendary studios, where artists like Bob Marley & the Wailers and Toots & the Maytals have recorded.

Bottom left: Major Lazer with Stephen McGregor, 2010. Stephen "Di Genius" McGregor is a young Jamaican dancehall producer who began making riddims at sixteen years old. He's produced and written songs with the most elite dancehall singers of Jamaica, including Mavado, Sean Paul, and Vybz Kartel. He is the son of the legendary reggae singer Freddie McGregor. *@DiGenius1*

Top right: Major Lazer with Busy Signal, 2010. Busy is one of the most well respected and active dancehall performers in the country. This photo was taken at his personal studio where he met with Diplo + Switch to record the vocals that ended up on the Major Lazer song "Sound of Siren." *@busysignal_turf*

Bottom right: Diplo with John Hill at Geejam Studios, Port Royal, 2010. John Hill is a producer + songwriter from New York. He and Diplo met while working on the first Santigold album. John has since worked with several major artists, including Shakira, Christina Aguilera, and Yoko Ono.

Lykke Li, recording with Diplo, 2010. Lykke Li is a singer-songwriter + artist from Stockholm.
She came to Jamaica at Diplo's invitation to record music over a three-day period in June 2010.
@Lykkeliofficial

Top: Fiction Lounge, Kingston, 2010.
Bottom: Anya Ayoung Chee, 2008 Miss Trinidad and Tobago Universe, 2009. *@AnyadeRogue*

JAMAICA
PLAYLIST

1. VYBZ KARTEL
   "Clarks"

2. ELEPHANT MAN
   "So High" (Owl City remake)

3. MAJOR LAZER
   "Pon de Floor"

4. DAWN PENN
   "No, No, No"

5. OPAL
   "I Said It!"

6. DAMIAN MARLEY
   "Welcome to Jamrock"

7. THE NOTORIOUS B.I.G.
   vs MILEY CYRUS
   "Party and Bullshit in the USA"

8. RDX
   "Bend Over"

9. DIPLO
   "I Just Wanna Fuck/Lady Gaga Mashup"

10. RIHANNA
    "Rude Boy" (TC remix)

Trench Town, Kingston, 2010. Home to Bob Marley, Trench Town was known in the sixties as a sort of Hollywood of Jamaica. Contrary to popular misconception, the neighborhood doesn't get its name

from a large open storm drain that runs alongside one of its main roads, but from an Irish landowning family who farmed there in the eighteenth century.

Above: View from Strawberry Hill, a hotel owned by Chris Blackwell, 2009. Known for its sanctuary-like environment, Strawberry Hill is located in Jamaica's Blue Mountains, north of Kingston, in the center of the country. Chris Blackwell was an incredible presence in the music business in its formidable years. He founded Island Records in 1959 and is credited with breaking artists such as Bob Marley and U2. For further reading on the label, pick up *The Story of Island Records: Keep on Running*, edited by Suzette Newman and Chris Salewicz.

Right: Rasta Chippy, a local who hangs out at Hellshire Beach, 2010.

Above: Dancehall style at Passa Passa, 2009.

Opposite: Girls in
white satin at
Passa Passa, 2009.

Above: Switch + Diplo at Tuff Gong Studio, working on the Major Lazer album.

UNIT
KING

ED
DOM

The United Kingdom is a great place for me to go. It's filled with many people I love, and I always meet someone new along the way. The country itself has been around for such a long time, but you forget how old it is when you're in London working. The UK has a deep musical history that you kind of feel everywhere. Music is really embedded in the country's spirit.

If Jamaica grows the ingredients for modern music, London puts it in the pot and turns up the heat. This is the place where music is initiated, scrutinized, experimented with, and refined. In London there are always five or six new genres coming out in a season. They all participate with each other and conversations about them can be heard on any Friday night. London has to be the most inspirational city for me. The backbone for distribution is parties and the BBC, the national public radio that promotes diversity and progression. If a song catches on there, it becomes ubiquitous. There's no bullshit—the British are honest and matter-of-fact, and that makes the place great to be in.

Previous spread: The Boiler Room, London, 2011.

Right: Pictured here are the yet unknown Oliver + Romy of the band the xx. They had a couple of days of studio sessions with Diplo right before the 2008 Notting Hill Carnival in England. The band has since gone on to sell almost a million albums worldwide and is celebrated within many aspects of music culture.

@thexxmusic thexx.info

Street fashion at
the Notting Hill
Carnival, 2010.

Opposite: Chris Mercer, professionally known as Rusko, performing in Liverpool in 2009. He is a premier DJ + producer and launched his career in the dubstep genre with his storming club single "Cockney Thug." Later, he was introduced to Diplo and signed to Mad Decent, where he has released one full-length album entitled *O.M.G.!* @*ruskoofficial*

Top: Diplo + Dillon Francis performing at the Boiler Room, 2011.

Bottom: Skerrit Bwoy on stage at the Notting Hill Carnival, 2010.

Top left: First Major Lazer show at the Notting Hill Carnival, 2008.

Bottom left: On the street at the Notting Hill Carnival, 2008.

Opposite: The Notting Hill Carnival, 2008.

Lee "Scratch" Perry in the studio with Diplo, 2010. In 1968 Perry wrote a song called "People Funny Boy." It was not only the first song in history to use a sample, but it also had a unique rhythm to it, which many consider to be the first known reggae rhythm. He produced a lot of Bob Marley's early tracks before he completely reinvented Jamaican music with dub. Dub is a sound created by adding reverb and fine-tuning drums and bass to get deep sounds, making the studio producer as much the artist as the musician playing the instruments. Jamaican immigrants who moved to the South Bronx brought these sounds with them and they became the catalyst for the invention of hip-hop.

Lee "Scratch" Perry
shows off some of
his accessories,
including his hat
(which he made).

On the following pages are portraits of DJs + producers: Fake Blood **(opposite)**, Drop the Lime **(top left)**, Boy 8-Bit **(top right)**, Sinden **(bottom left)**, and Jesse Rose **(bottom right)** at the Notting Hill Carnival in 2010. All of them uniquely contribute to the music that powers the club space in and out of the UK and the US. The music they create occupies various genres of house, electro, and new disco. @IamFakeBlood @dropthelime @boy8bit @gsinden @mrjesserose

Above: Skream, Manchester, 2009. Skream is considered by many to be the pioneer of dubstep. He started making records at the age of fifteen out of the UK garage scene. He had what is considered to be the first crossover dubstep song, "Midnight Request Line." He is one-third of the group Magnetic Man, along with producers Benga + Artwork. *@l_Skream*

UNITED KINGDOM
PLAYLIST

1. ## UK APACHI WITH SHY FX
   "Original Nuttah"

2. ## KATY B
   "On a Mission"

3. ## GYPTIAN
   "Hold Yuh" (Major Lazer remix)

4. ## JACK BEATS
   "Get Down"

5. ## BENGA & COKI
   "Night"

6. ## LA ROUX
   "Bulletproof"

7. ## SWITCH
   "This Is Sick"

8. ## STICKY FT MS. DYNAMITE
   "Booo"

9. ## DIZZEE RASCAL
   "I Luv U"

10. ## BURIAL
    "Archangel"

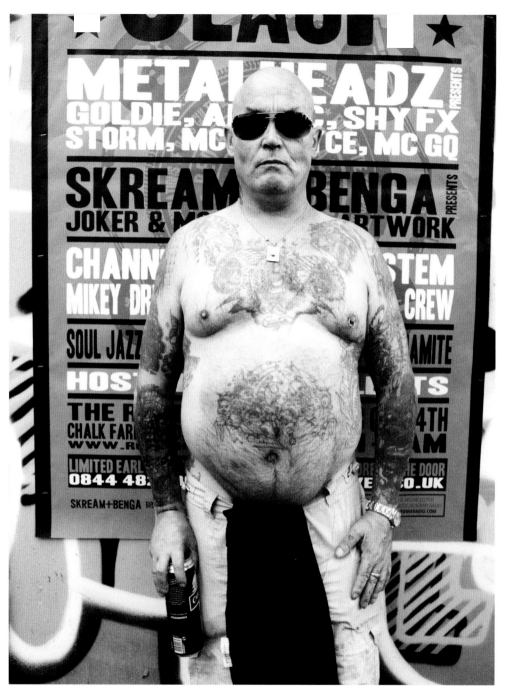

The Notting Hill Carnival, 2010. Starting its life as a local festival set up by the West Indian community of the Notting Hill area, it has now become a full-blooded Caribbean carnival, attracting millions of visitors from all over the globe. It is miles of colorful floats, traditional steel-drum bands, scores of massive sound systems, and tons of jerk-food stalls. In the evening, the floats leave the streets in procession, and people continue partying at the many Notting Hill Carnival after-parties.

Top: Diplo + Santigold on the mic, 2008. *@santigold*
Bottom: Chris Leacock, Nick Beith, Fake Blood, and Diplo, 2009.

Opposite: Concertgoer,
London, 2009.

Above: We went to his flat in the outer suburbs of London to work together on a few tracks. He plays in a jazz band and still attends university despite the fact that he is one of the biggest producers in dubstep at the moment. Recently Kanye West + Jay-Z sampled his "I Can't Stop" for a song on *Watch the Throne* entitled "Who Gon Stop Me." *@fluxpavilion*

Opposite: Joshua
Steele, aka Flux
Pavilion, 2009.

Top: Ben Geffin from Jack Beats, Nottingham, 2009. Jack Beats is a duo hailing from London, comprised of Geffin + Niall Dailly. They make progressive electronic music and have deep roots within hip-hop and UK grime. *@jackbeats*

Bottom: Fan with a rare Diplo vinyl, the Boiler Room, 2011.

Top: Second annual Major Lazer Carnival, 2009. From left to right: Paul Devro, Nick Veit (aka Nick the V), Maluca, Trini Chris, Diplo, and Jasper Goggins. This is a candid group shot of some of the Mad Decent artists. *@pauldevro @theV @MALUCAMALA @jillionaire @diplo @jaspergoggins*

Bottom: David Rodigan with Lee "Scratch" Perry, 2010. David Rodigan is an English DJ + radio host who has championed the sound of Jamaica for more than forty years, particularly in the United Kingdom. He is in many ways an institution, pictured here with reggae legend Lee "Scratch" Perry. *@rodigansreggae*

This shot is of Lunice from Montreal during a session at the Boiler Room in London in 2011. The Boiler Room is a unique performance setting in which DJs play for a studio audience and the set is broadcast live over Ustream. It's as close as you can get to MTV in real time. People interact with

the DJ set through chat and message boards. Lunice is an electro-hip-hop producer of French-Canadian descent. He resides in Montreal, where he began his foray into music through b-boy culture. *boilerroom.tv @Lunice*

Above: Shoreditch, a built-up neighborhood of inner-city London, 2011.

Opposite: Benga is an English DJ + producer of Nigerian descent. He is one-third of the group Magnetic Man and a frequent collaborator with DJ Skream. He is the writer + producer of "On a Mission," the Top 10 UK single by Katy B. He tours frequently and has released many influential songs within the dubstep and electronic-music landscape. *@iambenga*

Top: The Apollo Theatre, Manchester, 2009.

Bottom: Mark Ronson + Diplo, 2011. Mark Ronson is an accomplished producer + musician. He won a Grammy for Producer of the Year in 2007. He has worked with many artists over his career, including Amy Winehouse, Lily Allen, Q-Tip, and more. He has also released three solo albums under his own name. *@iammarkronson*

Above: Diplo + Luca Venezia, aka Drop the Lime, 2011, share a moment in the hallway of KOKO in London. Luca is the founder of the music collective and label Trouble & Bass from New York City. *@dropthelime*

Below: KOKO, London, 2011.

RUS

SIA

Moscow is the most unpredictable city in the world. Nothing seems to make sense there, and you don't understand how big it is until you leave the airport and drive across fifty miles of frozen metropolis—and you're still not downtown. My first gig there was in an old diplomatic building that was turned into a hotel for new diplomatic businessmen. The lobby was a hot goulash of Cuban and Mexican men in cowboy hats, hookers, Polish jazz musicians, and Russian mafia. The promoter told me that he couldn't list the party in *Time Out Moscow* because it would bring in too many unwanted folks. His promo was strictly word-of-mouth.

On our second trip, I was supposed to leave from London, but the promoter booking the travel never booked the flights. Shane was already there, and I had to call him and say that he might have a five-day vacation in Russia. My tour manager for Europe is a guy named John Ayers, and he was able to get us a flight the night before we had to be there. He booked us a gypsy cab the next morning, and we barely made it to Heathrow. Driving back into Russia, my promoter showed me where Proxy and the new young scene of electro producers are coming from. It's a bit nicer than a slum in the Bronx, and these kids are making music in a sort of military-industrial *Hoop Dreams* kind of way, in hopes of leaving this country with their dance sounds. The landscape of the clubs is dark, sexy, and clouded with smoke and top-shelf vodka. There's little that lends itself to Western culture. Saint Petersburg is even stranger and more frozen, and it's frighteningly beautiful. I finished my show there in a small warehouse at dawn by jumping into a cold pond in front of the rented country club that hosted the party.

Previous spread: View from the hotel in Moscow, 2010.

Right: Diplo performing to a packed house in Moscow, 2010.

Above: Saint Petersburg, 2010.

Above: Oleg + his son on the street in Moscow, 2010.

Opposite: John Ayers, my tour manager for Europe, with his gun holster, where he keeps his cash. Ayers is also an accomplished DJ + producer and touring the world in his own right. Brought up in Notting Hill (London's center for Caribbean culture), he has become well known for his reggae mash-ups and dub rhythms. *@jstarremix*

Katya (friend of Oleg) on the train from
Moscow to Saint Petersburg, 2010.

Nastya **(opposite)** and Katya **(above)**, friends of Oleg, in Saint Petersburg, 2010.

Above: Russian producer + DJ Masha Pirumova, aka DJ Sestra, in Moscow, 2010. She is a friend of Oleg's who DJs parties in Bali, Sri Lanka, Norway, and Switzerland.

RUSSIA
PLAYLIST

1. PROXY
   "Raven"

2. DIRE STRAITS
   "Money for Nothing" (Giant Bootleg)

3. BOY 8-BIT
   "The Suspense Is Killing Me"

4. ZOMBY
   "Strange Fruit"

5. THE BLOODY BEETROOTS
   FT STEVE AOKI
   "Warp 1.9"

6. CALVIN HARRIS
   "I'm Not Alone" (Doorly remix)

7. BONDE DO ROLE
   "Marina Gasolina" (Fake Blood mix)

8. CONGOROCK
   "Babylon"

9. BOYS NOIZE
   "Yeah"

10. SOULWAX
    "Krack"

Above: Oleg + Nastya napping during a three-hour trip between cities, 2010.
Opposite: Diplo asleep on the train before a show in Saint Petersburg, 2010.

Top: Swimming at dawn at the Vozduh Club, 2010.
Bottom: Girls kissing at a club in Saint Petersburg, 2010.

Opposite: Diplo playing
a two-hour set in
Saint Petersburg, 2010.

The landscape of clubs is dark, sexy, and clouded with smoke and top-shelf vodka.

Above: Red Square before dusk, 2010.

Above: Midnight in Saint Petersburg, 2010.

Opposite: Makhlif
Alexandrovna, clubgoer, outside
the Vozduh Club, 2010.

TRIN

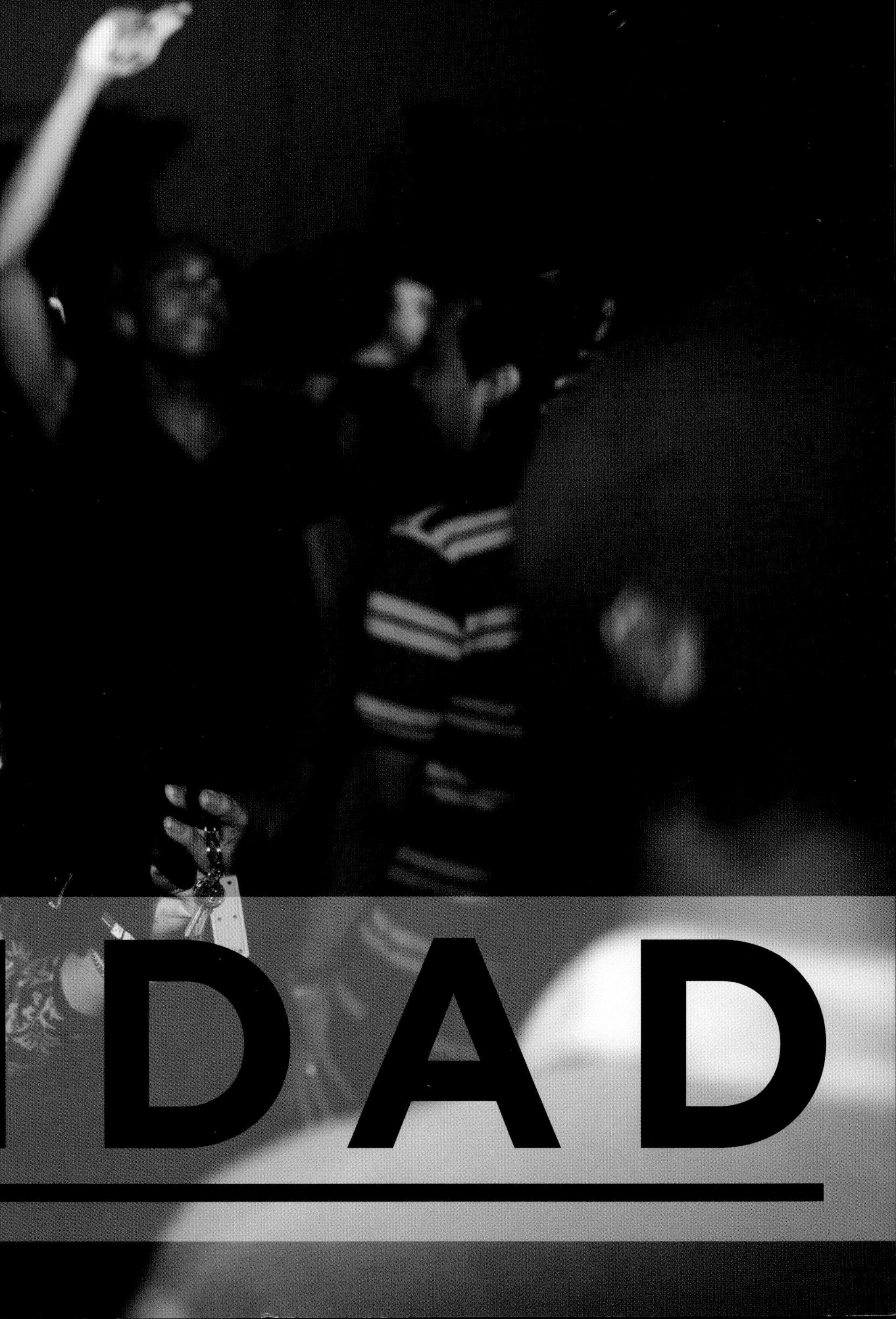
DAD

I wrote a column for *Vanity Fair* that took me to Trinidad for the annual carnival season. Carnival happens in many of the Caribbean islands as well as in London. Events generally run for three days and are twenty-four-hour celebrations of music, culture, local foods, etc. My first trip to Trinidad, I arrived from the West Coast with a terrible toothache and migraine. Chris Leacock picked me up from the airport at 5:00 a.m. with his off-duty police-officer cousin and a bottle of rum, and we headed out to the morning *j'ouvert* parties…no time to sleep on this trip.

There is probably nothing worse for a migraine than twenty-four hours of soca, a heavy carnival schedule, and driving straight into the countryside in the blazing equatorial sun. I've been in this game for a bit—I can party as hard as the hardest of them, but nothing prepared me for the madness of Trinidad during carnival season. Trinidad's mix of African, English, and Indian culture, which is split right down the middle, is something uniquely Caribbean. Everything revolves around curry, rum, and dancing. Machel Montano (the undisputed King of Soca) and Chris Leacock (the King of Weird Islanders) are the island's two international ambassadors. They've been great hosts to me and have made me feel like family every time I've been there. Our second trip had me showing my film *Favela On Blast* at a cinema on the island with one of the world's most famous artists, Peter Doig, a local hero of the art scene.

Previous spread: Miss Trinidad 2008, Port of Spain, Trinidad, 2009.

Right: Diplo + Chris Leacock, aka "Trini" Chris, Port of Spain, 2009. Leacock owned a bar in Port of Spain for a few years that hosted more progressive electronic music as well as traditional soca parties. He was Trinidad's ambassador for new DJ culture and brought Diplo to the island to play with Lil John. He now lives in New York and Los Angeles and DJs in the US. He occasionally moonlights as the hype man for Major Lazer. @jillionaire

Machel Montano, onstage, hosting a soca party in Trinidad. There are usually three parties a night, all outdoors. *@machelmontanohd*

Above: Chris Leacock, 2009.

TRINIDAD
PLAYLIST

1. ALISON HINDS
   "Roll It Gal"

2. M.I.A.
   "Galang"

3. MACHEL MONTANO
   "Floor on Fire"

4. DR. EVIL
   "More Punanny"

5. PATRICE ROBERTS FT
   MACHEL MONTANO
   "Band of D Year"

6. HOLLERTRONIX
   "Um Milhao"

7. NADASTROM
   "Save Us (aka Jacks Horny)"

8. CHELLEY
   "Took the Night"

9. CIARA
   "Ride"

10. LA ROUX
    "In for the Kill" (Skream remix)

Revelers at one of Machel's late-night soca parties.

Temple in the Sea, a well-known Hindu place of worship. Practicing Hindus pray, recite mantras, and plant flags on this site, located in front of a temple, which is off a pier in the distance.

The Hindus believe that their prayers and mantras will be carried through the flags and benefit all living things in the surrounding areas.

Above: View from Chris Leacock's car in Trinidad.
Opposite: Guest at Diplo's party in Peter Doig's art space.

Trinidad's mix of African, English, and Indian culture, which is split right down the middle, is something uniquely Caribbean.

Country road in Trinidad.

MEX

ICO

Being in Mexico is kind of everything you think it might be: It's dangerous, thrilling, wild, and unpredictable. Toy Selectah is one of my good friends from there. He introduced me to Calle 13 and other giants in the Latin music scene. Toy was in Control Machete, an enormous hip-hop group from Mexico that brought the culture to Latin America, and his A&R work was instrumental in bringing reggaeton to America. Mexico is like Israel in that there's a sense of risk on every trip out. The shows in Mexico go off. It's not like in the US either. The kids in Mexico are like anarcho-crust-punk-rave freaks. They also bootleg all your shit. On this tour, I remember that we made some shirts for the shows, and in Monterrey and Mexico City, the bootleggers had better shirts in cooler colors for sale outside of the club.

Previous spread: Mexico City, 2011.

Right: Diplo at sound check in Monterrey, 2011.

Opposite: Toy Selectah playing in Mexico City, 2011. An institution in Mexico, Toy currently lives in Monterrey and is one of the founding members of Control Machete, which has sold more than 500,000 albums in Latin America. Toy has been instrumental in introducing the Latin music underground to North America and was an early pioneer of the now-global sound of reggaeton. He is an active DJ + producer in Mexico and South America. *@ToySelectah*

Right: Diplo + Toy Selectah backstage in Mexico City, 2011.

Below: Diplo + Toy Selectah DJing the after-party of the Major Lazer show in Mexico City, 2011.

Above: A clubgoer at Blue in Mexico City, 2011.
Opposite: On the street in Mexico City, 2011.

Diplo + Mimi performing at Blue in Mexico City. Mimi is the full-time dancer for Major Lazer and is a winner of the Washington, DC, Dancehall Queen Competition. *@DHQMIMImjrlzr*

Above: Skerrit Bwoy "daggering" a girl
from the audience, 2011.

MEXICO
PLAYLIST

1. ERICK RINCON
   "Todos a Bailar"

2. DAVE NADA
   "Punk Rock Latino"

3. DUCK SAUCE
   "Barbra Streisand"

4. MUNCHI
   "Sandungueo"

5. KID CUDI vs CROOKERS
   "Day 'n' Nite"

6. DILLON FRANCIS
   "Masta Blasta"

7. DIPLO
   "Must Be a Devil"

8. HOT CHIP
   "Over and Over"

9. AURITA CASTILLO
   "Chambacu"

10. BRUJERIA
    "Don Quijote Marijuana"

Top: Skerrit Bwoy, 2011.
Bottom: Diplo DJing in Mexico City, 2011.

Opposite: Street style in Mexico City, 2011.

Being in Mexico is kind of everything you think it might be: It's dangerous, thrilling, wild, and unpredictable.

Mariana + Mercedes, local fashion designers, at the after-party for the Major Lazer show, 2011.

Skerrit Bwoy crowd-surfing in
Mexico City, 2011.

ASIA

A few years ago I did an extensive tour of Asia with my friend Steve Aoki. That guy, in and of himself, is probably the subject of an entire book, but for the purposes of space and time, I'll stay on topic! I have the best time in Asia. I've been to several of its countries. In Vietnam I played a party on a boat that had a circle slash for what you couldn't bring on board; the sign included cows and bazookas. I threw a grenade into a field, watched American propaganda, held a DJ workshop in Cambodia (it may have been Jakarta), and did karaoke on the fiftieth floor of a high-rise in Tokyo, among other things. The food is crazy and so, so good, and the scale of some of the cities, like Tokyo, Hong Kong, and Seoul, is just incredible. There are so many people stacked on top of each other, frantically moving, riding bikes, and trying not to get into a traffic jam with an elephant.

In most of Asia the music is just wild because it's hard to get there with a lot of frequency. There are certain countries in Asia that have a storied history of becoming independent, and some still exist in very harsh environments. For instance, Vietnam is a very new democracy, so if you're looking for local modern music, it's scarce and hard to find anything pre-1970s. I found a psych-rock record from 1968 that I was told was banned by the government at the time.

Previous spread:
Hong Kong, 2009.

Right: Diplo on
the Great Wall of
China, 2009.

Steve Aoki in Hong Kong, 2009. Aoki is a Los Angeles native and the owner of Dim Mak records, which he has been running since he was in high school. Originally heavily involved in the punk and hardcore scenes in California, he began DJing locally at a small club in Los Angeles called Cinespace

to support a weekly night that showcased live acts. Since then, he has started creating his own high-energy, party-atmosphere, lighthearted music, which has spread around the world. dimmak.com *@steveaoki*

Above: Diplo in Hong Kong, 2009.
Opposite: The streets of Hong Kong, 2009.

In most of Asia the music is just wild because it's hard to get there with a lot of frequency.

Entrance to the Forbidden City, Tiananmen Square in Beijing, 2009.

Above: On the way to the show in Hong Kong, 2009.

Opposite: Mimi dancing
with security in Beijing,
2010, at the culmination of
The Creators Project put
on by *Vice* and Intel.

Top: Departing from Manila, 2010.

Bottom: Kids running in the rain in Manila, 2010.

Opposite:
Butterfly knife
+ handcuffs,
Manila, 2010.

Above: Model Emi Matsushima in Tokyo, 2009. *@emimatsushima*

ASIA
PLAYLIST

1. ## CALVIN HARRIS
   "Bounce" (Micheal Woods remix)

2. ## AFROJACK
   "Bangduck"

3. ## LAIDBACK LUKE
   "Break the House Down"

4. ## PLASTIKMAN
   "Spastik"

5. ## MAJOR LAZER
   "Keep It Goin' Louder"

6. ## ANGGER DIMAS
   "Are You Ready" (Mahesa Utara remix)

7. ## FELIX CARTAL
   "The Joker"

8. ## GD & TOP
   "Knock Out"

9. ## SEDUCTIVE
   "Underground Sound"

10. ## SIDNEY SAMSON
    "Riverside"

Above: Diplo + Steve
Aoki in Tokyo, 2009.

Top: will.i.am and Diplo in Osaka, 2009. will.i.am of the Black Eyed Peas stopped by for the Diplo/ Steve Aoki show in Osaka after his group performed a stadium. He came to hang out and visit and ended up playing an impromptu thirty-minute DJ set. He and Aoki also performed Aoki's song "I'm in the House." *@iamwill*

Bottom: Steve Aoki French kissing a dog (not his), Tokyo 2009.

Opposite: Beijing, 2008.

Above: Driving through Shibuya in Tokyo, 2009. **Opposite:** Jesse Keeler + Al Puodziukaz of MSTRKRFT at Ageha in Shin-Kiba. MSTRKRFT are from Toronto, Canada, and during the Asian tour, they played a surprise set in Tokyo. Jesse is also in the duo Death From Above 1979 and Alex was the producer of that band. MSTRKRFT make electro dance music, whereas Death from Above 1979 had a more raw and visceral punk aesthetic. MSTRKRFT gained early attention in 2006 with a song called "Work On You." *@MSTRKRFTmusic @jfkmstrkrft*

UNITED

STATES

I was born in Mississippi and raised in Florida. I spent time in Tennessee, Alabama, and South Carolina, too. I never got settled, never was comfortable, never had an easy time in one place, but this helped to make me adaptable and it made it easy to maneuver. I shoplifted my first sampler from Sam Ash music center in Orlando, Florida. I was working part-time at Subway, learning to use a Dr. Rhythm Drum Machine and DJing house parties with vinyl records I'd accumulated from flea markets and mail order. Between rent checks, my turntables were always in and out of the pawnshops. Eventually I found a way out of Florida, got a scholarship to school, and went north to Philadelphia to try to crack the music scene.

After some years I made it on my own. I got checks from clubs, ran my own parties, and learned to produce and make music. Much of it was terrible but some of it was good. I traveled between Philly and New York, out to the West Coast, through the South, and into Canada. It was like a disease that spread out of Philadelphia. I feel like when we started to do Mad Decent and our parties locally, we didn't get much attention, but now we have the eyes of the world on what we are doing.

We met new kids making music, traded music with others, spread our ideas, and learned more about music here and there. I began to see the beginnings of a new scene and a new language, with kids making music and participating in the US music scene. I'm just trying to be part of this and to help to push some ideas out there a bit more.

New Orleans might be my favorite city in the US. It's strange and unpredictable—a complete mashup of the culture and history that represents America. But everywhere I go, I see the energy and the vibe in the US. It's the most exciting country to watch. Things here change quickly, and our history and variety are unrivaled.

Previous spread: Skerrit Bwoy dives into the crowd at the Pitchfork Music Festival in Chicago, 2010.

Right: Major Lazer record-release show in New York, 2009.

Top: Skerrit Bwoy backstage at Hard L.A., 2010.

Bottom: Major Lazer onstage at the Pitchfork Music Festival in Chicago, 2010.

Opposite: Elliot Aronow, editor of RCRD LBL and host of *Our Show with Elliot Aronow*. A New Jersey native and punk enthusiast, Aronow began his writing career at *Fader*. *@youngelz*

Top and bottom: Dave Nada at the Mad Decent Block Party, Los Angeles, 2011. Dave Nada and Matt Nordstrom make up the DJ duo Nadastrom. In 2010 Nada accidentally created a new genre of dance music called moombahton by slowing down a house record, which is traditionally 128, to 108 bpm, giving it a more distinct Latin-paced tempo. Since then, he has released a compilation CD of original moombahton on Mad Decent. *@davenada @nadastrom @mattnordstrom*

Opposite: Alexis Krauss of Sleigh Bells, a band consisting of her and Derek Miller. The duo resides in Brooklyn, New York, and makes metal-influenced punk music with programmed beats, bridging a unique gap between rock and dance. *@sleighbells*

Skerrit Bwoy at Hard L.A., 2010. Hard L.A. is a series of dance/electronic-music events that take place several times a year throughout the United States. Justice, Soulwax, Underworld, Moby, Daft Punk, and more have participated. It has evolved into a multi-day event with more than fifty thousand attendees. hardfest.com *@HARDFEST*

Top: Major Lazer + Crystal Castles at Hard L.A., 2010. Crystal Castles consists of Alice Glass, who joined the group at fifteen years old, and Ethan Kath of Toronto. Blending a raw, almost Gothic-punk vocal with searing electronic programming, they perform not as DJs but as a band with a live drummer. They have a subversive live show that is high-adrenaline in intensity. *@crystalcastless*
Bottom: Alexander Ridha, aka Boys Noize, at the Electric Zoo Festival in New York, 2011. Ridha is also the founder of the label BoysNoize Records. His sound is heavily influenced by techno and he is argu-ably the leader in innovative new music within that genre. From Berlin, he frequently collaborates with the clothing designer Wasted German Youth, whose direct design approach has informed much of the visual look of his music. He also produces other artists. boysnoize.com *@boysnoize*

UNITED STATES
PLAYLIST

1. M.I.A.
"Paper Planes"

2. RUSKO FT AMBER COFFMAN
"Hold On" (Sub Focus remix)

3. THE XX
"Islands"

4. HOLLERTRONIX
"Golddigger" (Tugboat edit)

5. CHRIS BROWN FT
BUSTA RHYMES & LIL WAYNE
"Look At Me Now"

6. MSTRKRFT
"Heartbreaker" (Laidback Luke remix)

7. KHIA
"My Neck, My Back"

8. BENNY BENASSI
"Cinema" (Skrillex remix)

9. BLAQSTARR
"Superstar"

10. BRENMAR
"Taking It Down"

Opposite: Major Lazer fans at Terminal 5 in New York, 2010. **Top:** DJ Ayres, A-Trak + Diplo at the Major Lazer after-party in New York, 2010. DJ Ayres is a staple in the world of New York DJs and makes up one-third of the fantastic DJ crew the Rub. *@djayres* **Bottom:** Nick Catchdubs, A-Trak + Diplo in New York, 2010. Nick Catchdubs is a former writer + editor for *The Fader*, a DJ, and a partner in A-Trak's label Fool's Gold. He is a music enthusiast and has hosted mixtapes with and for the likes of Mark Ronson and Wale. *@catchdini*

"WITHOUT MUSIC,
LIFE WOULD BE A MISTAKE."

—*Friedrich Nietzsche*